GAME DAY USA

NCAA College Football

SOUTHERN UNIVERSITY

Robb Kendrick

UNIVERSITY OF MICHIGAN

Sam Abell

R. Emmett Jordan

Rich Clarkson

UCLA

Douglas Kirkland

Kenneth Jarecke

■ SUGAR BOWL

Fans celebrate with wide receiver Dale Dawkins after the University of Miami's victory in the Sugar Bowl, which won them the national championship.

Bill Frakes/ Miami Herald

GAME DAY USA

NCAA College Football

produced by

RICH CLARKSON

the photographers

Sam Abell

William Albert Allard

Jose Azel

David Burnett

Rich Clarkson

Jay Dickman

Dan Dry

Bill Eppridge

Arthur Grace

Kenneth Jarecke

Lynn Johnson

R. Emmett Jordan

Nick Kelsh

Robb Kendrick

Douglas Kirkland

Brian Lanker

Neil Leifer

John Loengard

Michael O'Brien

George Olson

Jim Richardson

William Strode

the writers

Frank Conroy

David Halberstam

Richard Hoffer

Willie Morris

published by

The Professional Photography Division
of Eastman Kodak Company
and
Thomasson-Grant

Bill Marr	**Art Director**
Susan Vermazen	**Picture Editor**
Peter Howe	**Picture Editor**
R. Emmett Jordan	**Associate Producer**
Chris Adams	**Research**
Joe Bullard	**Editor**
Michael H. Rudeen	**Copy Writer**

■ NOTRE DAME VS. USC

Notre Dame drum major Keith Matherne whips the Irish band into fighting fettle during a pre-game performance on the steps of the Golden Dome, the school's administration building.

Rich Clarkson

Published by The Professional Photography Division of Eastman Kodak Company and Thomasson-Grant, Inc.
Copyright © 1990 by The Professional Photography Division of Eastman Kodak Company and Thomasson-Grant, Inc.
All Rights Reserved.

This book, or any portions thereof, may not be reproduced in any
form without written permission from the publishers.

Printed and bound in Japan by Dai Nippon Printing Co., Ltd.

97 96 95 94 93 92 91 90   5 4 3 2 1

Library of Congress Cataloging-in-Publication Data
Game day USA : NCAA college football / produced by Rich Clarkson ;
the photographers, Sam Abell ... [et al.] ; the writers, Frank Conroy ... [et al.].
p.   cm.
ISBN 0-934738-71-8
1. Football—United States—Pictorial works. 2. National Collegiate Athletic Association—Pictorial works.
I. Clarkson, Rich. II. Abell, Sam. III. Conroy, Frank. 1936–   . IV. Eastman Kodak Company. Professional Photography Division.
GV959.5.U6G36 1990
796.332'63'0973—dc20   90-33744

Thomasson-Grant
One Morton Drive, Suite 500
Charlottesville, VA 22901
(804) 977-1780

P r e f a c e

I grew up in a college town, and some of my earliest memories are of the Friday night rally before The Big Game. As the years passed, autumn became my favorite season, not so much for the games as for the football weekends.

Thus, my mind began racing ahead when Bob Sprenger, assistant executive director of the NCAA, began talking of game days in a planning meeting for the new Visitors Center.

"What I would love to see is a book called GAME DAY USA that captures something of everything that goes on," he was saying. What he spoke of was a book more about social behavior than sports, more about alma maters and memories than contracts and instant replays, more about anticipation and achievement than balance sheets and drug wars.

Right off, I knew how to make this book. Assemble a team of the best photographers and writers in America—none of them specialists in sports. As I began calling around the country, it was almost as easy as asking five-year-olds if they wanted a chocolate. Famous journalists reorganized schedules. I seldom got past the first explanation of what GAME DAY USA would be before being interrupted by, "Yes, count me in." It was 10 minutes into our planning before David Halberstam discovered he was to be paid.

After we insured that our look at GAME DAY USA included every area of the country, and after we included both large and small schools, the journalists selected their own subjects. Some chose alma maters, some the biggest rivalries in college football.

All were encouraged to bring back their own interpretations of the weekends they covered. The photographers edited their own film and presented the editors with personal visions. Some pictures make pointed statements, while others are documentary. There are photographs of uninhibited spontaneity and images from carefully orchestrated portrait sittings. There are moments of insight and high drama.

But mostly there is fun. For that is the substance of college football, and that was our hope for GAME DAY USA.

—Rich Clarkson

■ GRAMBLING VS.
TEXAS SOUTHERN

College football's
winningest coach,
Grambling's Eddie
Robinson, has led the
Tigers for 49 years,
sending in thousands
of plays, as here with
offensive guard
Charles Wilson. At
the end of the 1989
season, Robinson had
won 358, lost 124,
and tied 15.

Rich Clarkson

Introduction

GAME DAY USA is what college athletics is all about.

For me and for many of the people who follow college football, this book brings to life that special feeling we get when we walk into a stadium on a Saturday afternoon in the fall.

These images from some of the nation's finest photographers capture far more than the experience of the student-athlete. They encompass all that surrounds an autumn afternoon.

GAME DAY USA reaches into the personalities of college football. There are revered coaches: Bo Schembechler making his final charge into mammoth Michigan Stadium, flanked by his assistant coaches and his last roster of players; Eddie Robinson of Grambling, doing what he does absolutely the best—inspiring a young man to do his job better.

There are the funny hats and costumes of the fans and the painted faces in the student sections…the traditions of the alumni who wouldn't miss a Saturday afternoon at "their" place, with or without victory…the pain of defeat and the ecstasies of triumph on cheerleaders' faces…the determination and dedication of inspired marching bands…and perhaps best of all, the American flag, unfurled on a field of green in a picture that makes you almost hear the music of our anthem.

College football envelops all of us, young people, alums, fans, students, media, professors and administrators. Its spirit has the power to lead whole communities toward a common cause. Fall Saturdays embrace all of these constituencies, and that flavor of college football is what satisfies me most about intercollegiate athletics.

Most of all, for those of us involved in teaching and coaching the young people of America, game day is the time when athletics and academics come together. In featuring all of the people who create the excitement of intercollegiate athletics, GAME DAY USA shows how the NCAA aims to combine "student" and "athlete."

—*Richard D. Schultz*, NCAA Executive Director

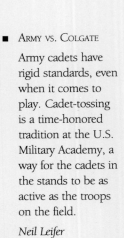

■ ARMY VS. COLGATE

Army cadets have rigid standards, even when it comes to play. Cadet-tossing is a time-honored tradition at the U.S. Military Academy, a way for the cadets in the stands to be as active as the troops on the field.

Neil Leifer

following pages

■ COLORADO VS. NEBRASKA

University of Colorado assistant coach Gary Barnett erupts when the team doesn't score on a short-yardage play. On the next down, CU scored against Nebraska, giving the team a lift on its drive to the Orange Bowl.

R. Emmett Jordan

■ NOTRE DAME vs. USC

It's easy to believe
that Notre Dame is
in divine hands,
especially as fans hurry
to the stadium on a
crisp fall day during a
winning season.
Thousands clog the
main campus on game
mornings, munching
fresh-grilled ham-
burgers, crowding into
the bookstore and
listening to the band
concert.

Rich Clarkson

Army cheerleader Christine Juhasz falls toward the waiting arms of her partner. In 1989, the Army relaxed its hair-length restrictions, allowing women cadets to wear longer hair with the condition that it is pinned up for ceremonies and other special occasions.

Neil Leifer

■ YALE VS. HARVARD

The collegial spirit
prospers at Ivy League
games, especially
during the annual
Bulldog-Crimson
contest.

John Loengard

By David Halberstam

n the fall of 1949 when I was 15 years old and callow and unsure of myself, I visited my brother in Cambridge during the Harvard-Princeton weekend. Sometime late that morning the Harvard University Band, more than 100 members strong, started playing a miniature concert in the middle of Harvard Yard. Then, neatly dressed in crimson blazers, dark grey slacks, but no pomp, no Ruritanian motorcycle-escort hats, they started marching through Harvard Square on their way to the Lars Andersen Bridge and Harvard Stadium.

I fell in behind them, completely enchanted. They were wonderful, they radiated confidence that they were the best in the world at what they did (and they probably were), and one manifestation of this high and exalted sense of their excellence was their individualism: They cared not one whit about being in step. That was what first struck me: They were brilliant at what they were doing, and they were all out of step.

They were marvelously hip, though one had not yet come upon the word *hip*. I was utterly drawn to their style, or perhaps even better, their anti-style. Other bands marched with precision, employing rigidly perfect moves, not an eyelash out of synch. The Harvard band by contrast was incoherent: There was at best a kind of communal shuffle. They broadcast by their style, by their body language (a phrase we did not have then), that they were very good and that they were very irreverent about being very good. They did not have to employ precision drill techniques to impress us. All we had to do, their body language seemed to say, was listen. Princeton crunched Harvard that day, and somewhere in my memory there is a small note that they scored more than 60 points. I remember little of the game; what I remember is the band and the fact that *that* was the moment I decided I wanted to go to Harvard.

If there is something that sets apart Ivy League football it is that *hip*. In the world of hip, the strong and powerful do not triumph—they are in fact doomed to fail. It is the cool and knowing who win. Thus almost everyone who opts for an Ivy League education, football player and regular student alike, makes a choice very early on in which football prowess and football success are somewhat peripheral. These are not football powers. The entire nation does not await the game on Saturday afternoon. Keith Jackson, stocked to the brim with clichés ("That big fella can really lay a hit on you") is not in the broadcast booth. Yet the Ivy League has its own wondrous celebration, and Saturday is important. The football itself is good, better than most outsiders think. (The Ivy League schools, one Big Ten recruiter said, can kill you on a certain kind of bright and talented high school player you badly want. You offer them a chance to play on national television a few Saturdays a year, he added, but those damn Ivy League recruiters, who are the pillars of their communities, can offer them a place in their law firms.)

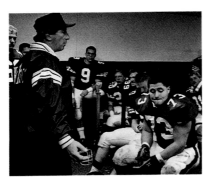

John Loengard

What makes the celebration special is not just that it is irrevocably linked to tradition (after all, Harvard started playing Yale some 105 years ago), but that those who celebrate are absolutely sure that they are going to run the country in 25 years. At many schools thousands cheer because their players are going to a bowl game. In the Ivy League fans cheer because they believe that they are going to the National Security Council. That defines the proportions. (In my senior year, Dick Waldron, my roommate, was the head cheerleader. On the morning of the Yale game he woke my other roommate and me and said with great delight, "Do you know what day this is?" We admitted that we did not. "This is the last bleeping time I have to cheer is what day it is," he said.)

The game matters, the sport matters, but above all the celebration matters. It is an event and an occasion of bonding. If we are not that good at this, the unwritten code seems to say, then it is only because we are so much better at things that truly matter.

No one would dare go to an Ivy League school and, at a rally, talk about the Need For School Spirit. Spirit is as spirit does, and spirit is mostly free. ("How we will celebrate our victory/we will invite the whole team up for tea," Tom Lehrer wrote in "Fight Fiercely Harvard.") I have a classmate named Stan Katz who is today the head of the American Council of Learned Societies, one of the most prestigious jobs in academe. While still an undergraduate Katz proclaimed Katz's law: Princeton fans, he said, cheer loudly for a touchdown. Yale fans cheer loudly for a first down. But Harvard fans often cheer loudest over vantage points. That is, the people at the south end of the field would cheer wildly if Harvard or the other team (it seemed not to matter) had the ball within the 10-yard line at the north end of the field and the clock ran down at the end of the first or third quarters. They were cheering because the action was coming to their end of the stadium. It was Katz who reminded me of another Harvard cheer during the Dartmouth game when Dartmouth was ahead. The Crimson fans shouted out the score and then in unison added in one great volley: "Now Tell Us Your SAT Scores!"

John Loengard

But for all of that, for all of our being a part of the celebration and yet mocking it, we were for the first time in our lives part of a wonderful pageant. It is almost 40 years since I was a freshman, and over the years those games have blended, scores have faded from memory, yet the colors of the Saturday have become if anything sharper: the huge crowds across the field in blue (coats, jackets, sweaters, scarves) for Yale or orange and black for Princeton or green for Dartmouth. At the Harvard Crimson before each game we had a Puncheon/ Luncheon—a pre-game lunch at which we ate and drank, and to which the visiting editors of the other daily were duly invited to join us. We did, though we did not admit it, show our style, our plumage and the plumage of the ladies with us, which was a critical part of our own plumage, though we were loathe to admit it. There is in all of it a wondrous, early sense of belonging to something larger.

I think that is what mattered. It was football, but it was never about football. It was about belonging. We had applied to these venerable schools, once the exclusive property of only the aristocracy, and they had, much to our surprise, accepted us. But for a long time we were not of them; we went to class, we discreetly (almost covertly) displayed the tiniest symbols that would identify us—the closest thing to an announcement of membership was the color of our scarves. But we did not yet feel that our place was rightful. Indeed we probably doubted it. This was Harvard (or Yale or Princeton), but did we really belong, were we truly part of it? It was, first and foremost and most readily, on those fall Saturdays when we could have it both ways (participate, be cool, cheer, but cheer almost mockingly), that we belonged for the first time, and as such became part of something larger.

■ YALE VS. HARVARD

Harvard fans try to light a fire under their team's partisans, while the Yale band drums up support with a play on Harvard's motto, *Veritas* (Truth), versus Yale's motto, *Lux et Veritas* (Light and Truth).

John Loengard

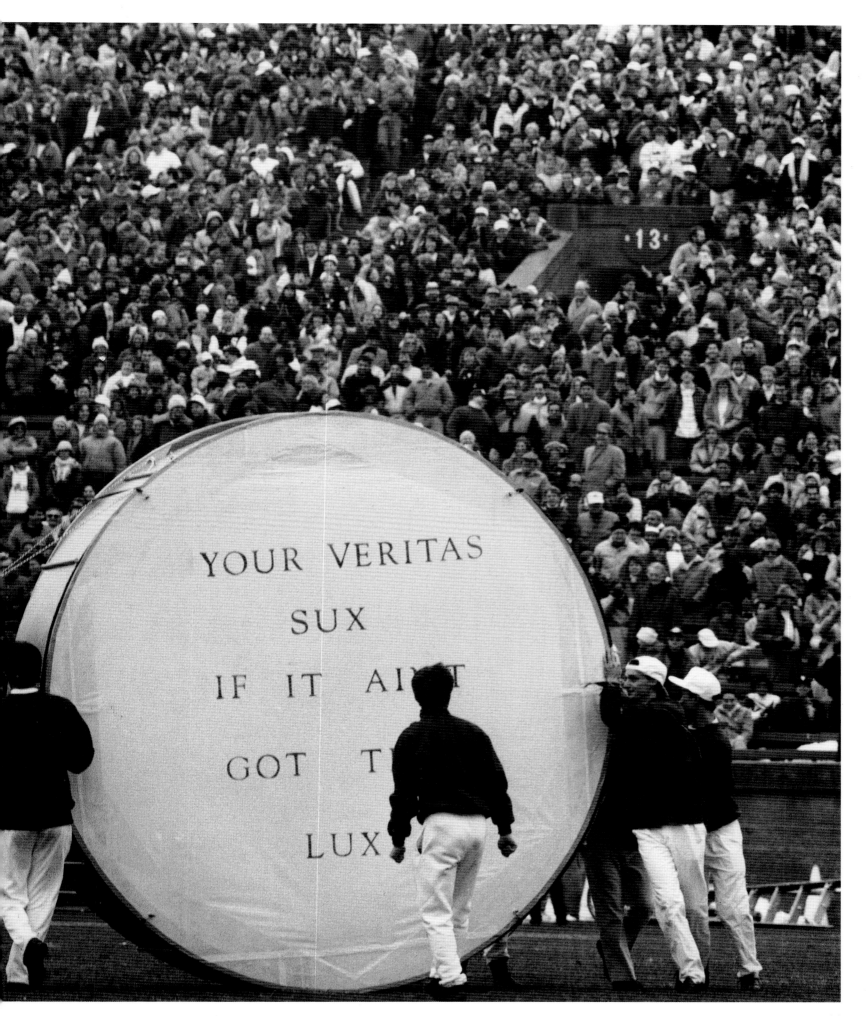

left

■ Yale vs. Harvard

Jayne Chen, class of
1990, plays cymbals
for the Harvard band.
"She was just part of
a wonderful ethnic
mix that prevailed at
both schools," said
photographer John
Loengard; "it was
striking in comparison
to the traditional Ivy
League WASP-ness.
The stands looked
like something out of
a 'Benetton World'
commercial."

John Loengard

above

■ Yale vs. Harvard

When asked, "Would
you rather go to
Harvard or be dead?"
handsome Dan XIII,
the latest in a long
line of bulldog
mascots, drops to
the ground, feigning
death. Some of his
predecessors were
passive, hardly able
to summon up the
enthusiasm to bark
at a game. Others
were retired to a
farm because they
were too vicious.

John Loengard

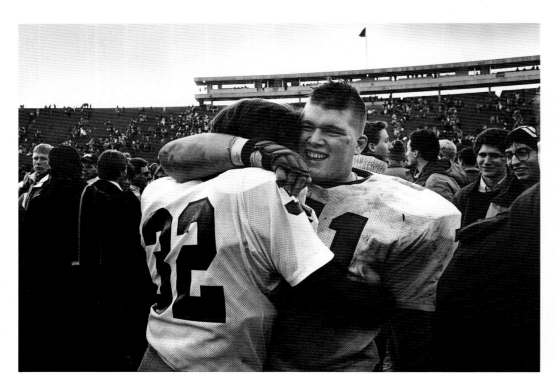

■ YALE VS. HARVARD

Nothing is emptier than a football stadium after a game, especially when you're a Yalie and your team has lost once again to Harvard.

John Loengard

■ NORTH DAKOTA STATE
VS. AUGUSTANA

College football
players are larger than
life to their young fans,
who relish an oppor-
tunity to exchange
not-so-high fives with
their idols at North
Dakota State.

Nick Kelsh

■ HOWARD VS.
FLORIDA A&M

At many schools, the
band outshines the
football team. The
Florida A&M band,
here led by drum
major Julius Wilson,
pioneered such
techniques as high
knee-lifts and faster
marching cadence.
They were the sole
American band to
march down the
Champs Élysées as
part of the celebration
of the 200th anni-
versary of the French
Revolution.

Neil Leifer

39

Across America, the hours before kickoff may be as important as the game itself. Tailgating has become an autumn tradition that ranges from pre-game meals served on station wagon tailgates to elegant feasts served with caviar and candelabra on the aft deck of a motor cruiser. Terry Shumard, who sets a table at the Harvard-Yale game every year, says, "This is a celebration of what has been good over the years at schools like Yale. It's continuity. We celebrate the education and athletics at a good school—and it's a good excuse to bring good friends together."

above

■ STANFORD VS. CAL

At Stanford, the Indians banner is a throwback to another spirit—the school changed its team name to Cardinal in response to protests by Native Americans.

George Olson

right

■ WASHINGTON VS. ARIZONA STATE

Husky fans combine tailgating with a day at the lake, arriving at games via Lake Washington and docking their cabin cruisers next to the stadium. Kayaks are sure to find a parking space.

George Olson

■ PENN STATE VS. ALABAMA

Penn State's rabid fans motor in from all corners of the state for Saturday games. Later, 83,370-seat Beaver Stadium will be as crowded as the camper-only parking lot.

David Burnett

It's easy to find a
parking spot at North
Dakota State games,
especially if you arrive
early. The wide-open
space says more about
geography than about
the football team,
whose winning ways
often earn them a trip
to the Division III
playoffs.

Nick Kelsh

Tailgating Ivy League
fashion is a celebration
of style as well as
sport. Terry and Libby
Shumard (backs to the
camera) prepared beef
tournedos, lobster
bisque, caviar appe-
tizers and champagne
for their friends Stan
and Dorothy Klein
before the game. The
year before, bitter cold
caused the shrimp to
freeze in the cocktail
sauce and the cham-
pagne bottle to
explode in its bucket
—but the Shumards
set another table in
1989 for their 15th
annual tailgate party.

John Loengard

■ COLORADO VS. NEBRASKA

The Colorado team's charge onto Folsom Field is led by a 1,400-pound female buffalo, Ralphie III. With the handlers struggling to keep up, Ralphie intimidates opposing teams by dashing down the sidelines.

R. Emmett Jordan

■ ALABAMA VS. AUBURN

Fans wear their emotions on their sleeves (or sweat shirts) in rivalries as intense as Alabama-Auburn, usually played at Birmingham's Legion Field, a "neutral" site. In 1989, students from each school wore their messages for the first meeting at Auburn's Jordan Hare Stadium. More than 85,000 packed the stadium and college town, population 28,471.

Bill Eppridge

■ STANFORD VS. CAL

"The Big Game" is no news to Stanford students, who pretend to read copies of the student paper and chant "boring, boring" while Cal's band is on the field.

George Olson

Photography by Jose Azel

The furthest point east in the United States where major college football is played is Alumni Stadium in Orono, Maine, home of the Maine Black Bears. There, coach Tom Lichtenberg fashions a team in a setting that is both big-time and quaint. The furthest outpost in the Yankee Conference, Maine must travel south and west to every road game, as they did here to Boston University. The Black Bears thrive on a regimen of discipline and the tradition of "The Hammer."

■ During the six-hour bus ride to Boston, the Walkman becomes part of the traveling uniform. On game morning, coach Tom Lichtenberg leads his players on a 20-minute walk. When they return to the hotel, he holds the door open and greets every player by name.

■ Military regalia is part of the uniform at Maine, that and "The Hammer," a trophy given to the special teams player—here, cornerback John Ballard—who fired the best shot in the previous week's game. The motif carries over to the special teams meeting, where coach John Baxter, a military enthusiast, gets his troops ready to hit the beach.

■ Tailback Carl Smith rests after having raced 42 yards to a touchdown with only a minute left in the first half. His score put Maine back into a game that was not going well. In the crowded visitors' locker rooms, assistant coaches assembled players in the shower area to plot a better second half. Smith, a Division 1-AA all-American, ran for 169 yards on the day.

■ The favored Black
Bears were not playing
well, and offensive line
coach Mike Pendino
(left) and head coach
Lichtenberg attempted
to motivate their
players as the game
wore on. But the day
would not end in
victory—a field goal
attempt fell short as
time ran out.

■ PENN STATE VS. ALABAMA

The early bird gets
the best parking spot
outside Beaver
Stadium, named for
James A. Beaver,
former Pennsylvania
governor and, more
important, president
of the Penn State
board of trustees.
These fans parked
their vans and trailers
the night before the
game, and Penn-
sylvania had a new
city—for one night.

David Burnett

following pages

■ NEBRASKA VS. OKLAHOMA

Football fever is a
lifelong affliction for
Nebraska fans like
the Snodgrass twins,
who come to Lincoln
every game day from
South Omaha.
Cornhusker season
tickets are sometimes
bequeathed in the
wills of Nebraskans.

Kenneth Jarecke

61

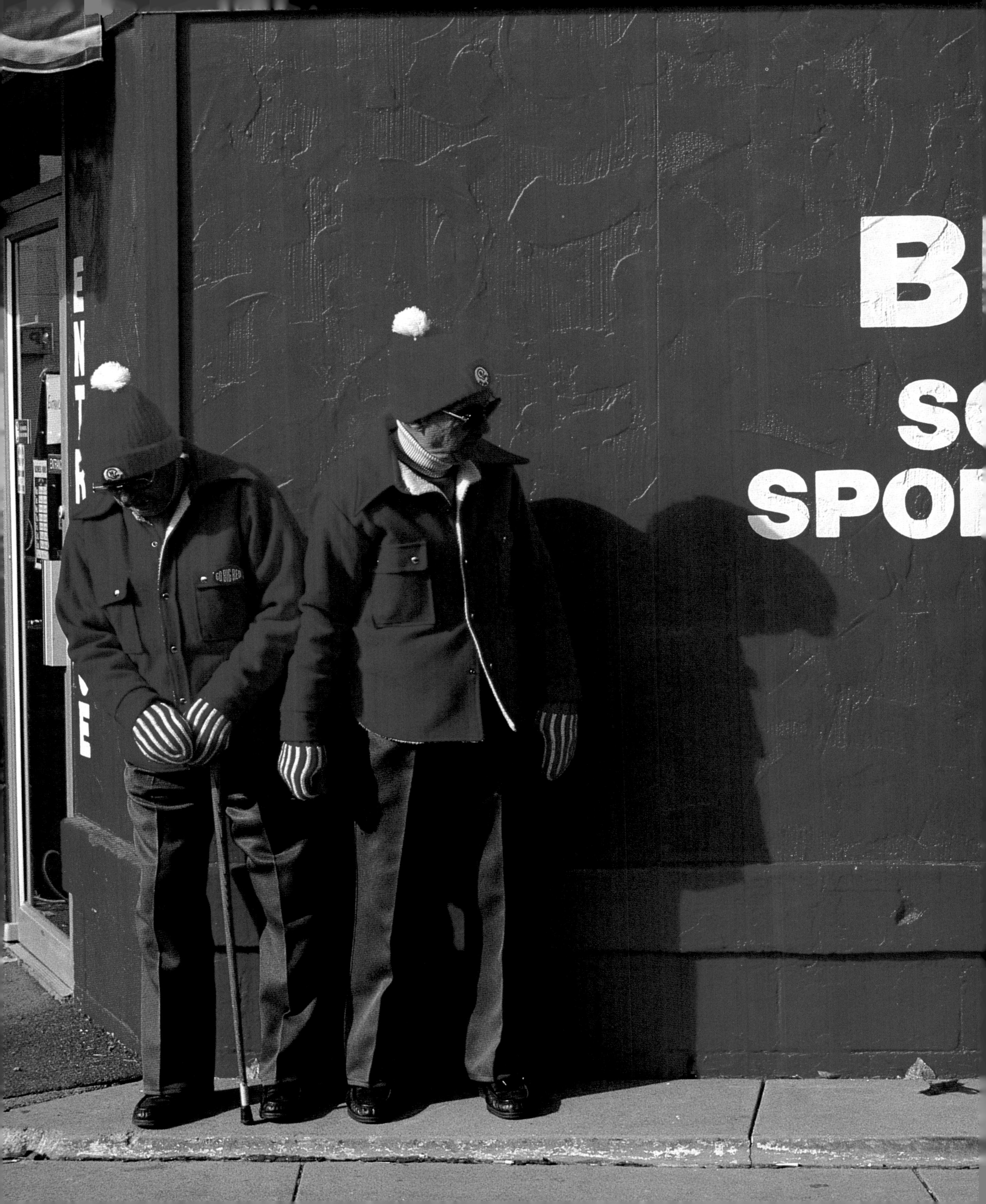
GO BIG RED

G RED
UVENIR &
TING GOODS

■ EASTERN NEW
MEXICO STATE VS.
WEST TEXAS STATE

When the West Texas
State Buffaloes travel
from their Canyon,
Texas, campus, so
does their bison
mascot, along with
a crew of handlers
and a custom truck
and trailer.

Michael O'Brien

65

■ MISSISSIPPI VS. VANDERBILT

In the center of the
Ole Miss campus,
"The Grove" is home
to ritual tailgate
parties under the huge
oak trees.

William Albert Allard

By Willie Morris

This is a tale not of one Game Day but two, because each was deeply enmeshed in the other.

It begins with the Ole Miss-Vanderbilt game of October 28, 1989, in Oxford, Mississippi. It was Ole Miss Homecoming, one of those Southern autumn days touched with the airy bittersweet languor of the past and memory and childhood...and football.

Ole Miss is small by measure with other state universities, with 10,000 students—roughly the same population as the town—who are suffused with the flamboyant élan of their contemporaries everywhere. In moments there is a palpable, affecting sophistication to its stunningly beautiful campus in the rolling rural woodlands of the South.

On this homecoming day, one might recall Thomas Wolfe's only slightly fictional Pulpit Hill, patterned after the Chapel Hill of many years ago in *Look Homeward, Angel*: "There was still a good flavor of the wilderness about the place—one felt its remoteness, its isolated charm. It seemed to Eugene like a provincial outpost of great Rome: the wilderness crept up to it like a beast."

Two hours before the kickoff, the young men of the Ole Miss team, led by coach Billy "Dog" Brewer, walked single file through the Grove, a huge old verdant circle only a stone's throw from the stadium, as avid tailgaters applauded. From the distance the band played "From Dixie with Love," a blended rendition of "Dixie" and "The Battle Hymn of the Republic." As the mighty sounds wafted across this wooded terrain, little girls in the school's Harvard red and Yale blue tossed and leapt, and miniature quarterbacks in replica jerseys threw footballs to incipient Rebel wide receivers. The adults were drinking, and everywhere was the ineffable cachet of fried chicken and barbecue. On one lengthy table draped with a vintage Delta tablecloth were eight-branch silver candelabra with red tapers and mounds of food on matching silver trays. On another was a substantial arrangement of flowers flowing out of an Ole Miss football helmet—lacy white fragile baby's breath and red carnations.

The stadium itself, surrounded by young magnolias, was cozy and contained, and much removed from the mega-stadiums of the SEC behemoths Alabama, Tennessee, Georgia, LSU and Florida. Its grassy turf had seen Bruiser Kinnard, Charlie Conerly, Barney Poole, Jake Gibbs and Squirrel Griffin, Gene Hickerson, Archie Manning and Gentle Ben Williams.

There were 34,500 in attendance on this afternoon, including a smattering of Vandy partisans down from Tennessee in their bright gold colors matching the golden patina of this day. The *New York Times* would report of what was to follow: "The game blends into the dense history of a school that has often played out the richest and darkest passions of the region."

William Albert Allard

There is a special flavor, a texture, to Deep Southern collegiate football, and this was best expressed years ago by Marino Casem, the long-time coach at Alcorn University:

> In the East college football is a cultural exercise. On the
> West Coast it is a tourist attraction. In the Midwest it is
> cannibalism. But in the Deep South it is religion, and
> Saturday is the holy day.

There was indeed a religiosity to this mingling crowd in the moments before game time. In the south end zone a loyalist group perennially regarded as The Rowdies, a perfervid cadre consisting of professors, bartenders, writers and reprobates, shouted epithets at the visitors down from their cerebral Nashville halls: "Down with the Eggheads! Stomp the Existentialists!" A Yankee reporter, surveying this end zone phalanx, asked one of its number, Dean Faulkner Wells, niece of the hometown bard, why she supported Ole Miss football. With a succinctness uncharacteristic of the Faulkner Breed, she replied: "Continuity."

The record of the Ole Miss team at this juncture was five wins, two losses. They were hobbled with injuries. At one point the entire starting defensive backfield was down, including football and academic all-America safety Todd Sandroni, who today was playing on one good leg. The Rebels' largest margin of victory had been seven points. They had upset Florida on the road by four while gaining only 128 offensive yards. They had defeated Georgia on a touchdown pass with 31 seconds to go in this stadium, and Tulane on another pass in New Orleans with four seconds remaining. It was a funny, gritty ball club, small and hurt in the mighty SEC, a ball club people could not help but love.

There was 6:57 left in the first quarter when it happened.

Vandy faced third and goal from the Ole Miss 12 in a scoreless game. Quarterback John Gromos faded for the pass. Brad Gaines, the 210-pound fullback, caught it on the two.

William Albert Allard

Roy Lee "Chucky" Mullins, 175-pound Ole Miss cornerback, suddenly raced across the field, leapt high, and tackled the receiver, forcing him to drop the football. The resounding thud could be heard for yards around. Cheers rolled across the stadium. But Mullins lay prone on the field, and when he did not move a fateful quiet descended.

"I couldn't get off the sideline," Ole Miss coach Dog Brewer would later recall. "In all the years I've been coaching, it's the first time I haven't gone on the field when there was a serious injury. I couldn't go. I thought the kid was dead. No matter how long I coach, I'll always remember how he came flying through the air and made that hit—the thud of it."

The silent throng watched as the trainers and doctors cut Mullins' face mask away and strapped him to a wooden board. It took more than 10 horrible minutes. They carried him to the opposite sidelines, and the ambulance slowly wound its way out of the stadium toward the hospital. The scene would not easily be obliterated.

The rest of the first half seemed bitter anticlimax. The flat, listless Ole Miss team fell behind 10-0. Chucky Mullins' injury likewise cast an ominous pall over the homecoming rituals of halftime, the Ole Miss beauties in evening dresses, the playing of the Alma Mater.

How to explain such human moments? Ole Miss came out in the third quarter on fire, then erupted in the fourth. Trailing 17-16, Ole Miss took over on its own 21 with 9:18 remaining. Halfback Tyrone Ashley carried twice for 13 yards, then quarterback John Darnell hit tight end Rick Gebbia of Long Island ("our own Yankee") for 49 yards to the Commodore 17. On the ensuing play, Ashley broke free for the winning touchdown with 7:18 left. The game ended 24-17.

In the locker room the Ole Miss players were choked up over their fallen teammate. There was no celebration.

Sometime in the second half Chucky Mullins had been flown to Memphis, 75 miles away. The small hospital in Oxford could do little but stabilize his condition. He lay now in neurosurgery intensive care in the Baptist Memorial Hospital.

He was paralyzed from the neck down. The injury was serious, with little likelihood that he would ever recover. The attending doctors would call it one of the most dramatic injuries they had ever seen, likening the impact that crushed his back to the crushing of an empty can. The vertebrae had exploded; there was nothing left. On the Monday after homecoming, four surgeons performed a three-hour operation using wire and a bone graft from Chucky's pelvis to fuse the shattered vertebrae. He would remain a quadraplegic.

The mood of the university, the town and the state in the following days was of grief and sadness. Ole Miss dedicated the rest of the season to him.

In 1987 Chucky Mullins, a 17-year-old from the tiny town of Russellville, in northeast Alabama, came to Ole Miss, one of many poor young blacks signed each year by the Rebels. When he was recruited and given an athletic scholarship, he did not have the money to get to Oxford. His mother had died when he was six, and his father not long after that. He was raised by a legal guardian, a young man who suffered from a debilitating lung disease. In his senior year in

Bill Eppridge

high school, Chucky was the football captain, and his team won the state championship. Both Auburn and Alabama considered him too small and slow, and he wanted to go to Ole Miss.

He was Dog Brewer's kind of athlete: "He was lanky, always clapping, having fun, what we call a 'glue' player, not that fast or big, but the kind that holds a team together. What you saw him wearing was damn near what he owned. But to see him, you'd think he was a millionaire."

Chucky's best friend on the Ole Miss team was a white freshman named Trea Southerland. After Chucky's operation in Memphis two days after the Vandy game, he came out of the anesthesia whispering Southerland's name. "Chucky added a lot to other people's lives," Southerland said. "And I know that if desire and character make a difference, he'll find a way to beat this."

A chance photograph before the Vanderbilt homecoming game had caught a pristine moment. Coach Brewer and Mullins are standing together in the north end zone, not far from where Chucky would soon be hurt, the coach's arm around number 38's waist as the two of them lead the team onto the field. It was a gesture of symbolic affinity: Brewer was also from a poor family and a broken home, attending Ole Miss in its glory days as a "step slow" ball player. "When you love the game, it has a hold on you," Dog says of Mullins, but it is an autobiographical confession too. "I kind of saw myself in him. The only way out for both of us was football."

Ole Miss was matched the next Saturday against the Bayou Bengals of LSU. For the first time since 1961, this tumultuous and historic rivalry would be played in Oxford.

Within hours of Chucky Mullins' injury a trust fund had been started for him. LSU collected donations at its Purple-Gold basketball game in Baton Rouge. The University of Delaware shut down a football practice an hour early for a prayer session. Calls from coaches—and the White House—came from all over America. Coach Bill Curry of Alabama collected donations from his players.

Rich Clarkson

71

Brian Lanker

"Statistics tell us," Curry said, "that football is a very safe game when you're talking about catastrophic injuries. Ankles? Knees? Fingers? No, it's not safe. But not one time in a billion do you see the kind of injury that happened to Chucky Mullins."

Mike Archer, the LSU coach, visited Chucky in the hospital Friday night before the Saturday game. "I can understand how this affected their team," he said. "I almost broke down with tears when I visited with him. It hurts to see a strong, healthy kid like that, so young."

Shortly before the game, seven young white Ole Miss men in the final for "Colonel Reb," the campus' highest accolade, withdrew from the election and swung the honor to Mullins.

The LSU match would be one of the most dramatic moments in Ole Miss sports annals. The Rebel players wore number 38 on their helmets. The largest crowd in the history of the little stadium, 42,354, turned out for the contest. Hundreds of Ole Miss students volunteered to pass buckets during the game for the trust fund. More than $240,000 would be collected at this game, five times more than the goal.

Chucky Mullins was listening to the radio in the intensive care unit in Memphis. Just prior to the kickoff there was a prayer for his welfare.

The Vandy victory the previous Saturday had given 6-2 Ole Miss an opportunity at the SEC title and a chance at its first Sugar Bowl since 1970. Yet devastation struck the Rebels early, and it was obvious that they were taut with emotion—fumbles, incomplete passes, penalties. LSU quarterback Tom Hodson was magnificent, and the Tigers jumped to a swift 21-0 lead. The score was 35-10 late in the third period, and the LSU depth was showing.

Then, suddenly, as they had all year against adversity, the Rebels, outweighed and outmanned at nearly every position, crippled by injury and despair, came alive in the final quarter. Quarterback Darnell's formerly errant passes began to click, and slashing runs by sophomores Randy Baldwin and Tyrone

Ashley left gaping holes in the Louisiana phalanx. The Rebel players were yelling to each other after each big play: "This one's for Chucky! We're gonna do it!"

The score was now LSU 35, Ole Miss 30. The Rebels were driving from their own territory as the game ebbed away. A burnt orange sun was descending behind the Vaught-Hemingway Stadium, and the air was eerie with the early dark. The entire assemblage was on its feet, and the partisan fans were stomping in unison, filling the afternoon with the pandemonium of fealty.

Twenty-five seconds remained now, and the Rebels had first and 10 on the LSU 30. Quarterback Darnell, injured five plays before, limped back onto the field. An uncommon hush descended, and a member of the South End Zone Rowdies fell out of a lower row of the bleachers.

George Olson

As the play unfolded, Darnell hobbled back into the pocket. The nimble wide receiver, Willie Green, streaked toward the south end zone, covered only by cornerback Jimmy Young, four inches shorter. It took only seconds. The ball was in flight now, suspended it seemed for the briefest eternity etched against the waning hour, as Willie Green leapt high, arms outraised in one quick pirouette of hope.

The pass came up two feet short. The Bayou Bengals defender, high in the air with Green, intercepted in the end zone, then fell lovingly to the turf, ball in breast.

If the Rebels had scored, they would have led 36-35 with 20 seconds left. Going for and making the two-point conversion, they would have achieved a symbolic 38, the number they wore on their helmets for their stricken teammate.

Yet life often does not work that way. A great sporting event indeed emulates life, its ecstasies and sorrows, its gallantries and failures, and its time running out, the time that runs out in Dixie autumn twilights for all of us who wish life to give us feeling and victory and hope against old mortality. The Bayou Bengals intercepted, twenty seconds left. Only the love remained, and the possibility.

Photography by Robb Kendrick

■ Southern trombone players hustle through the band's "fast cadence"—a blistering 360 steps per minute —while playing and moving in intricate, dancelike formations.

More than 65,000 people crowd New Orleans' Superdome for what has become one of America's most amazing football weekends—The Bayou Classic between rival Louisiana schools Grambling and Southern. The game itself is only one part of a weekend that includes reunions, parties, rallies and two nights on the town in the French Quarter for both students and alumni. And most of the action occurs when the schools' marching bands square off in their own spirited competition.

above

■ At halftime, Southern's "Dancing Dolls" await drum major Gerrold Banks' signal to begin, and Faith Hunter, a marketing major, is crowned Grambling's Bayou Classic Queen.

right

■ Grambling's band even changes uniforms for part of their show. Director Conrad Hutchinson, Jr., trains the band to produce "the marriage of precision drill, tempo and dance steps— all while playing."

■ Grambling's drum
majors must have
both athletic ability
and poise, while
members of the
eight-man cymbal
unit must be strong
and tall enough to
perform intricate
behind-the-back and
between-the-legs
cymbal crashes.

Since 1973, the game has been played in the Superdome, where air conditioning is not enough to match the intensity. Grambling defensive tackle Henry Blades (right) and his team took home the trophy this year.

■ After the game comes
a night in New Orleans,
and on every floor of
almost every hotel,
parties abound.
Members of the Omega
Psi fraternity pose while
other fans head to the
French Quarter.

■ AUBURN VS. ALABAMA

Even the state's biggest rivalry can't hold the interest of all the people all the time.

Bill Eppridge

■ SMU vs. Rice

The Rice game was the first game in three years for the Southern Methodist University football program, which had been given an NCAA "death penalty" probation. Student managers and trainers, like most of the players, had never participated in an SMU game. Uncertainty was in the humid air. And new head coach Forrest Gregg, a former SMU star who returned to his alma mater from coaching the Green Bay Packers, was as nervous as his youthful team.

Rich Clarkson

■ VIRGINIA VS.
VIRGINIA TECH

The party started
immediately after
Virginia defeated its
intrastate rival on the
way to a 10-3 season.

Sam Abell

GALLAUDET

Photography by Lynn Johnson

The first surprise at a football game played by Gallaudet, a college for the deaf, is how similar it is to a game involving hearing players. Then the differences crop up: the national anthem signed, not sung; an enormous drum signaling by vibration the start of each play; the hasty signing between coach and players. The most significant difference, however, is how much everyone—players, coaches and fans—really communicates. People who communicate by signing must look closely at each other; that and shared experience seem to bring Gallaudet players and fans closer together.

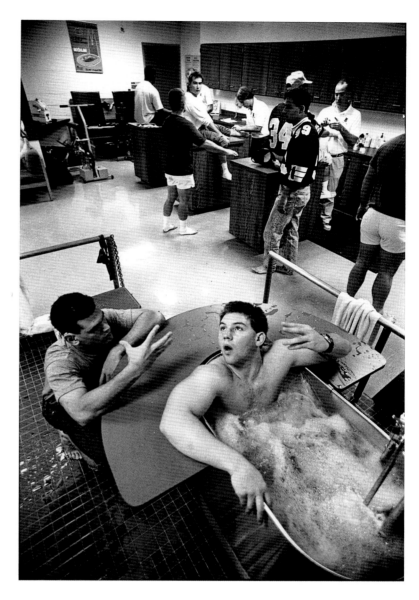

right

- Quarterback Jim Segala signs with a trainer at the whirlpool, and guard Joe Fresolo, Jr., watches a coach's instructions.

left

- Gallaudet players crowd around head coach Rich Pelletier, who is also deaf, making the sign for their team mascot, the bison.

■ The pre-game prayer, Gallaudet-style, is a moment of individual reflection. "Even though football is such an aggressive, physical and sometimes violent sport, there was always time for caring among the Gallaudet players," said photographer Lynn Johnson. "They were very close with each other, sharing common bonds, needing each other's support."

■ Communication at Gallaudet takes many forms: a student strikes a massive drum to signal the start of each play (players feel the vibration through the earth), and coach Pelletier signs his instructions on the bench. Following the game, split end Jeff Hubbuch and tight end Ralph Vernon share in Gallaudet's victory.

■ Post-game activities at Gallaudet are basically the same as at any school: some public, like the traditional shower for the coach, and some private, meant to be shared just by two. After the game, equipment manager David Culhane and girlfriend Gina Giancarlo cuddle in the Gallaudet drum, and quarterback Segala embraces his nephew on the sidelines.

■ WASHINGTON VS.
ARIZONA STATE

On Friday nights, the
Husky band meanders
through the campus,
serenading the frater-
nity houses and dorms,
attracting students to
the quadrangle for a
pep rally. Trombone
players began a tradi-
tion of adorning the
slides of their horns
with Husky bumper
stickers. The fad
caught on, and now
they have permanent
elastic covers for their
instruments.

George Olson

■ TEXAS A&M VS. TEXAS
On the night before
the annual game with
Texas, a group of
A&M students known
as the Redpots builds
and lights a bonfire
so high it made the
*Guinness Book of World
Records* in 1967 at 105
feet. The ceremony,
accompanied by the
school band and the
reading of a poem
dedicated to the
seniors' last game
against Texas, recalls
A&M's roots as a
military academy.

Rich Clarkson

■ WASHINGTON VS.
ARIZONA STATE

Greeks at Washington
pride themselves on
homecoming decora-
tions and often follow
the judges from house
to house. Some are
elaborate, like Theta
Chi's, which featured
a Sun Devil effigy that
was set afire, then
extinguished by a
"cloud" fed by a hose
and moved on a pulley.

George Olson

■ Notre Dame vs. USC

Amid the colors of
fall, fans gather
around student food
vendors on the Notre
Dame campus.

Rich Clarkson

THE MIDWEST

By Frank Conroy

The people who live here call it The Heartland—that agricultural region of the Midwest that includes Iowa, Nebraska, Kansas and vast stretches west of the Mississippi—and in many ways the name seems apt.

Certainly the national interest in sports can be seen here in its purest form, as an expression of regional pride, as a celebration of the power and beauty of youth. Not youth in the abstract, but in the actual sons and daughters of farmers, bank managers, teachers, combine operators, lawyers, real estate brokers, fertilizer salesman, auto mechanics, chiropractors and everybody else who lives here. Sports here are bound to family and community. They are not Roman rituals imposed from above to divert the populace. Their heady energy bubbles up from below as a distillation of the liveliness and vigor of the people themselves.

It is a journalistic truism to say that the most passionate fans are found in those communities with the most trouble—the once-great but now decaying and confused cities of New York, Detroit, Los Angeles—as people cling to whatever thread they can grasp of a social fabric that is coming apart. Perhaps that passion has a dark side. Football riots in England as an expression of despair, frustration and economic hopelessness. Fist fights and belligerent drunkenness at Yankee Stadium in a city torn by racism. Certainly it can have a dark side. But in The Heartland the fans seem truly to come together, to infect each other with their enthusiasm and hope, much as they might, in a very different way, in church. There doesn't seem to be a great deal of pain in the stands out there. Elation, disappointment, but all of it in scale somehow. All of it against the background of an enormous, open-ended, everybody-welcome public celebration. A party, in short. It's supposed to be fun, and it is.

Jose Azel

Iowa City, a university town whose population increases 25 percent the day before a game and 50 percent on the day itself. Thousands of cars, pickup trucks, vans and Winnebagos converging from all directions on Kinnick Stadium. Route 90, Route 380. Route 6, and every county road bringing people in from all over the state. From 30 miles away. From 300 miles away. Eighteen hundred and seventy-three motel rooms on the Coraville strip! Welcome to the Home of the Hawkeyes! Go Hawks!

People show the colors, and the colors are yellow and black—the yellow of corn, perhaps, and the black of the deepest and richest topsoil on the face of the planet. Yellow and black banners and pennants, yellow and black jackets, sweat shirts, running suits, socks and sweaters, decals and bumper stickers. Yellow and black banners in the shop windows and restaurants all over town, with the logo of a hawk, whose fierce gaze suggests swiftness and single-mindedness. The hawk is a powerful symbol in this kind of open country, where on any given afternoon you might see one gliding high over the fields and gently rolling hills, imperious and free in the air, patrolling its vast domain. The hawk, and the eye of the hawk, which can spot a mouse from 500 yards.

Yellow and black are the colors of the eye of the hawk. Even the buses in Iowa City are yellow and black. The truck stop out by the interstate highway is called the Hawk-I. The whole town is decked out. Everybody gets into the act. This is us! the colors seem to say. Here we are, by God!

On game day the visitors are everywhere. Most people don't even bother to try to park near Kinnick, where the lots are bound to be full, or where you can pay an enterprising householder 10 bucks for a piece of his front yard. Paying 10 bucks to park rubs Iowans the wrong way, tantamount to lighting up a cigar with a flaming bill. (Actually, $10 goes a long way in Iowa. A case of Rhinelander, a perfectly good underadvertised beer imported from Wisconsin, sells at the Econo Foods for $6.48. It moves particularly well on football weekends.)

Vehicles cluster up at different places around lunchtime. A large group from Cedar Rapids is over in City Park taking advantage of the public barbecue pits, the benches and tables where they set out spreads of potato salad, corn dogs, pickled eggs, chips and homemade cakes and pies. People eat from paper plates and clean up after themselves. Ten or 12 families from Davenport traditionally gather in the university parking lot beside the river, tailgates down, the kids busy feeding the ducks. Farmers from North Johnson County join up in the old practice field near Manville Heights.

Jose Azel

After lunch people lock up their cars and start drifting toward the stadium, converging from all points of the compass, ambling over the river on the bridges and footbridges (even the old railroad bridge), strolling along the streets and paths into the thickening crowd. Pre-game announcements from the PA system can be heard echoing in the crisp air. Band music floats like invisible smoke. A walk into emotion, because the closer you get to the field, the more charged the atmosphere.

By the time people get inside they are pumped. They look around at their fellow Iowans and a sense of well-being overcomes them. This is it! This is the day, the time and the place, and here we are together and powerful. Soon we will roar, and it will be strong enough to raise the hairs on the back of your hand. It will be deep enough to be heard a mile away, and it will arch over everything like a hawk in the sky.

In The Heartland some things remain relatively simple: the pleasures of coming together; the confirming power of common ritual; the affirmation of decency and fair play, of self-respect and hard work. It's all still here, tacit and modest most of the time, but truly celebrated on game day. The spirit of the people lifts every action, and every action lifts the people.

■ MICHIGAN VS.
OHIO STATE

The annual Michigan-
Ohio State game often
determines the Big
Ten's representative in
the Rose Bowl. As the
faces of these Buckeye
fans attest, this
afternoon was to be
Michigan's.

Rich Clarkson

■ BRIGHAM YOUNG VS.
OREGON STATE

At Brigham Young
University, the view
of the Wasatch
Mountains from the
press box offers
competition for the
events on the field.

Jim Richardson

117

■ NORTH DAKOTA STATE
VS. AUGUSTANA

Every Friday following
the last practice before
a game, North Dakota
State's offensive and
defensive coaching
staffs square off in a
touch football game
affectionately known
as the "Toilet Bowl."

Nick Kelsh

■ CLEMSON VS. WAKE FOREST

Soon after they enter
the stadium, Clemson
players stake out squares
of turf and study the
game program.

Dan Dry

■ Clemson vs. Wake Forest

Soon after they enter
the stadium, Clemson
players stake out squares
of turf and study the
game program.

Dan Dry

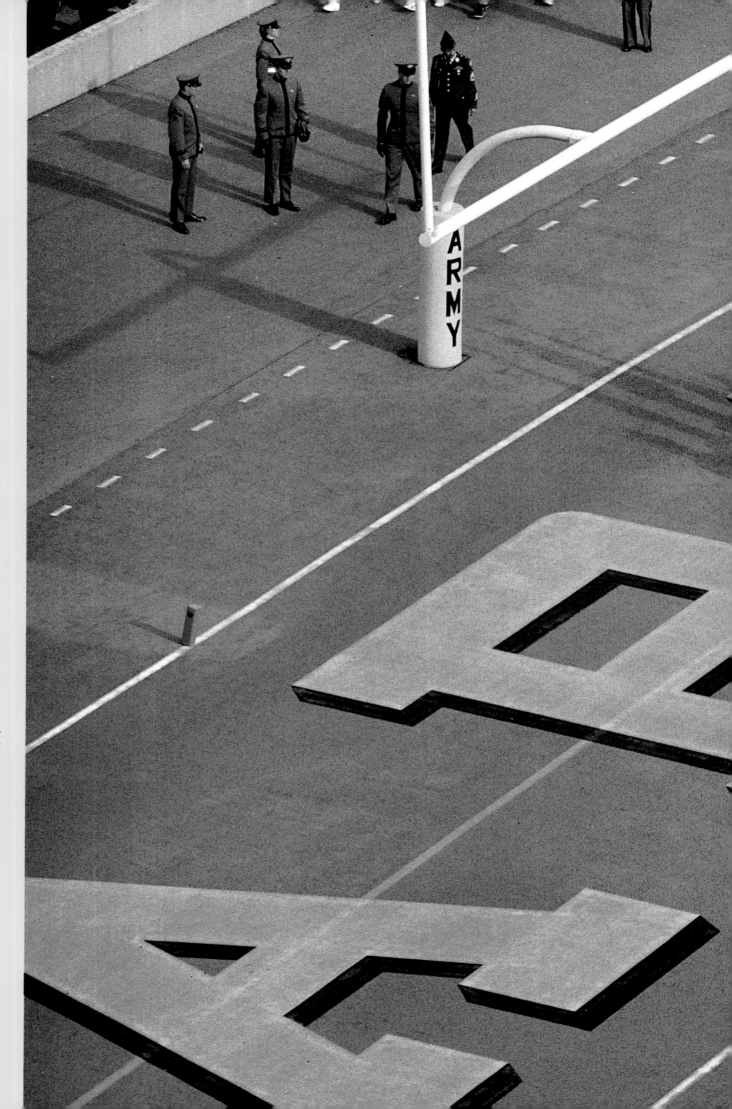

■ ARMY VS. COLGATE

At West Point, the cadet color guard prepares to take center stage for the playing of the national anthem. This ceremony and the pre-game "Parade of Cadets" on the Plain are part of the 100-year tradition that is Army football.

Neil Leifer

120

LOCKER ROOMS

Photography by Rich Clarkson

■ BOSTON COLLEGE
VS. TEMPLE

Before the game,
locker rooms are
quiet places, where
players talk in hushed
voices. As Boston
College teammates
stretch on the floor
before taking the
field, no one speaks.
When they walk
through the door
onto the field
moments later, the
same players shout
with enthusiasm,
and the traditional
slap of hands against
the door jamb
adds a final gesture
for luck.

Ever since Knute Rockne—or Ronald Reagan—exhorted the Notre Dame team to win one for the Gipper, The Locker Room Speech has been a big part of college football folklore. What actually happens behind those closed doors is as varied as the personalities of the coaches. Illinois' meticulous and highly organized John Mackovic outlines the day's objectives almost as if in a boardroom. Kansas' Glen Mason exhorts his team with the enthusiasm of an evangelist. Many coaches consider their locker rooms to be the most private of all inner sanctums—the door is closed to all outsiders. In all locker rooms before the big game there is great tension, some apprehension, and a seemingly unending wait.

"In the season, you get to play 11 times—if you play good enough, 12 times. Right now, we've got one, maybe two left. Seniors, you've got none left after this at Kyle Field. In this lifetime, you won't ever go out and do this again—take every minute of it, enjoy it, savor it, and play so you'll remember it. Two years ago, it came right down to the end of the ballgame. We sack 'em on fourth down and win the game. Seniors, you have a lifetime to think about the outcome. I'm telling you, you have 60 minutes to go out there and make it come out the way you want."

—*Texas A&M coach R. C. Slocum*

■ TEXAS A&M VS. TEXAS
Assistant coaches have their own pre-game jitters, but when coach R. C. Slocum has his final words for the team, the attention is all his.

"There is a legacy here at Grambling. You need to know about the legacy coach Robinson has created through all these years. Be proud you are a part of it. Coach used to tell us to aspire to come back to Grambling after our achievements. Then, he would stop the practice for the player to address the team. Today, I ask you what Coach once asked me: 'Someday, will you stop practice?'"

—*Buck Buchanan*

■ GRAMBLING VS. TEXAS SOUTHERN

After many nervous moments of waiting, coach Eddie Robinson and his team take in some final words before the game from all-pro alumnus Buck Buchanan.

"Now look...first play of the game, gadget play, touchdown! First play of the game last year, first play of the second half, double pass, touchdown! Now let's not let 'em get a cheap one on us today. Let's play every snap with discipline. Do you know what discipline means? That means do your job! Do your job, don't do somebody else's. The last team that Temple beat was in this room. No way this year! Let's not have any cheap ones today! Now, let's go."

—Boston College coach Jack Bicknell

■ BOSTON COLLEGE
VS. TEMPLE

Boston College's Jack Bicknell moves with his shouting and cheering team towards the field of Alumni Stadium. During halftime, quarterback Willie Hicks takes off his shoulder pads and jersey for a tense and quiet rest by his locker.

129

■ DAYTON VS. UNION

When Dayton played for the NCAA Division III championship in Phenix City, Alabama, the tiny locker rooms wouldn't hold the team. So coach Mike Kelly (left) and his team met with the specialty coaches behind the ESPN television truck. Dayton defeated Union (N.Y.) 17-7 to win the Amos Alonzo Stagg Bowl.

■ Illinois coach John Mackovic goes through a carefully crafted game plan before playing Indiana in the season's final home game.

"We should never wait for our opponent to dictate the tempo of the game—to see how he is going to play. We should go out from the opening whistle and dictate the tempo by how we play. How we cover the opening kickoff—the first series of downs."

—*Illinois coach John Mackovic*

■ Facing perennial Big Eight powerhouse Oklahoma, Kansas coach Glen Mason fairly shouts into his players' faces, trying to convince them they are capable of an upset victory.

"You have one obligation and that is to play hard. Your best effort—don't expect any more and don't settle for any less. I wanta' tell you something—we do all the things we've talked about and we come together as a team, we gotta' chance. Above all else we WILL be an enthused football team today!

—*Kansas coach Glen Mason*

■ COLORADO VS. ILLINOIS

Colorado fans, prophetic in their body paint considering the Buffaloes' eventual trip to the Orange Bowl, frequently take a casual approach to their game-day attire.

R. Emmett Jordan

■ SMU vs. Rice

SMU students celebrate the first season played in on-campus Ownby Stadium in 41 years. During the team's hiatus under an NCAA "death penalty," the stadium was renovated for the Mustangs, who had played at the Cotton Bowl or Texas Stadium since the 1940s.

Rich Clarkson

■ NOTRE DAME vs. USC

The young men of Notre Dame's Irish Guard march through the campus before every game. Each member must be at least 6 feet, 2 inches tall to reach 8 feet in full regalia, which includes bearskin hats and kilts. The kilt's plaid is registered in Ireland for Notre Dame's exclusive use.

Rich Clarkson

■ NOTRE DAME VS. USC
Wearing their distinctive Trojan battle garb, the University of Southern California marching band enters the stadium in South Bend, Indiana. The band, with Hollywood close to home, makes many nonfootball appearances, and once performed and recorded with rock band Fleetwood Mac.

Rich Clarkson

■ WASHINGTON VS.
ARIZONA STATE

His hat crowded with
symbols of loyalty,
a Washington Husky
fan encourages his
team to "mush."

George Olson

■ STANFORD vs. CAL

Members of the
Leland Stanford Junior
University Marching
Band personalize
their own standard-
issue hats to reflect
their sentiments.

George Olson

The term "pageantry" long ago became a cliché associated with college football, but like most clichés, it has more than a flash of truth. Everyone is on the stage—players, band members, cheerleaders, coaches, trainers, vendors, fans—beginning long before the kickoff and ending well after the final gun. At a bad game, it gives you something to watch; at a good game, it gives you something extra to watch.

■ MISSISSIPPI VS. VANDERBILT
All performers, including this Mississippi majorette, have to fight pre-game jitters.
William Albert Allard

■ AIR FORCE VS.
NOTRE DAME

An impending storm
notwithstanding, it is
a cheerleader's job to
get the Falcon fans
exercised. Cadets take
the encouragement
more literally: They
run to the end zone
each time the
Academy scores and
match their team's
cumulative point total
with pushups.

R. Emmett Jordan

■ MISSISSIPPI VS. VANDERBILT

In her room at the Phi Mu sorority, Margaret Pryor, 1989 Ole Miss Homecoming Queen, prepares for a day of parades and ceremony.

William Albert Allard

■ NORTH DAKOTA STATE
VS. AUGUSTANA

In a hallway near the
Bison locker room,
cheerleaders help each
other prepare for the
halftime performance
in Fargo, North Dakota.

Nick Kelsh

following pages

■ PENN STATE VS. ALABAMA

During halftime,
Penn State's dance
group "Orchesis"
sways to the rhythm
of rock and roll.

David Burnett

■ PENN STATE VS. ALABAMA

"A Touch of Blue," the 17-girl Penn State majorette line, performs with the band in their pre-game and halftime shows.

David Burnett

■ USC VS. UCLA

UCLA cheerleaders fly high in the Los Angeles Coliseum, home stadium of crosstown rival USC and site of the 1932 and 1984 Olympics.

Douglas Kirkland

■ NORTH DAKOTA STATE
VS. AUGUSTANA

In Fargo, where
Dacoteh Field is home
to the North Dakota
State Bisons, cheer-
leaders practice the
night before the game.

Nick Kelsh

■ BRIGHAM YOUNG VS.
OREGON STATE

Cougar cheerleaders
stay earthbound
but enthusiastic as
BYU pulls ahead of
Oregon State.

Jim Richardson

above

■ PENN STATE VS. ALABAMA

Hours of practice and sophisticated planning lead to fast-paced halftime shows. One of the nation's most organized bands, Penn State's Marching Blue Band practices at sunup Saturday for their afternoon show.

David Burnett

below

■ MICHIGAN VS. OHIO STATE

The tradition of Big Ten bands lives when Ohio State and Michigan meet in late November. Here, the disciplined Michigan band finishes its pre-game show with their "birthday cake."

Rich Clarkson

right

■ STANFORD VS. CAL

America's most outrageous—and perhaps most fun— band performs before its fans. For this show, the Stanford Dollies, including Mary Gehan (left) and Juli Oh, wear classic flapper dresses of the 1920s.

George Olson

above

■ TEXAS A&M VS. TEXAS

Members of A&M's "12th man" kickoff coverage team are nonscholarship players who practice with the team but only get into games briefly. They often pitch in to lead cheers from the bench.

Rich Clarkson

right

■ NOTRE DAME VS. USC

As leaden clouds move across the historic Notre Dame Stadium, the ebb and flow of the game is seen on the faces of the Irish cheerleaders. Here, with the clock running down, Notre Dame had just lost the lead. Moments later, Kristin Komyatte and her fellow cheerleaders would rejoice, for the Irish won in the last minute.

Rich Clarkson

■ WASHINGTON VS.
ARIZONA STATE

Autumn and football
go together—probably
never more than in
the vests fashioned by
these University of
Washington students.

George Olson

153

■ DUKE VS.
NORTH CAROLINA STATE

Ever wonder what happens to a goal post after it is torn down? Old-fashioned wooden goal posts were broken up as souvenirs, but metal posts have made that impossible. So these Duke fans, after their team had won 35-26, jumped onto the field, tore down the goal post and carried it from Wallace Wade Stadium and across the campus. And then not knowing what to do with it....

Arthur Grace

154

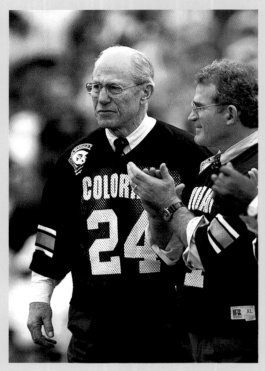

■ COLORADO VS. NEBRASKA

Returning to his alma mater to attend the Colorado-Nebraska game, Supreme Court justice Byron "Whizzer" White, wearing his old jersey number, was inducted into the university's all-century team.

R. Emmett Jordan

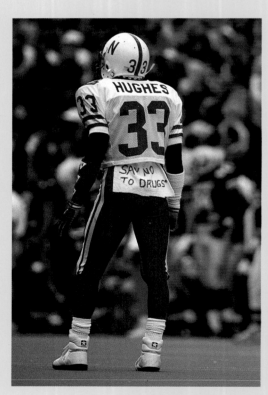

■ COLORADO VS. NEBRASKA

Nebraska wingback Tyrone Hughes displays his own message on a towel during the game that decided the Big Eight championship.

R. Emmett Jordan

■ COLORADO VS. NEBRASKA

Following Colorado's victory, the parties began at midfield before spreading across Boulder. Later, the Buffaloes would be ranked number one in the nation before losing to Notre Dame in the Orange Bowl.

R. Emmett Jordan

COLUMBIA

Photography by Arthur Grace

Columbia's city campus provides a setting for football unlike any other in the nation. The team's record is also unlike any other—six wins to 97 losses over the last decade. Despite the team's record and Manhattan's disinterest in college football, games still provide fun for the band, the fans—and even the Columbia players.

■ COLUMBIA VS. DARTMOUTH
Though the jumping drum major and the kicking cheerleader do their part, football is not a big attraction at Columbia.

159

above

■ CLEMSON VS. WAKE FOREST

Human mascots, it seems, have it tougher than the four-legged variety. Clemson's tiger, like the Air Force cadets, does pushups after each Clemson score, one for each cumulative point. In one game during Clemson's 1981 championship season, the team scored 82 points; the mascot did 465 pushups and lost nine pounds.

Dan Dry

right

■ TEXAS A&M VS. TEXAS

The only activity Reveille 5, the Texas A&M mascot, is known for is howling during games. The collie is kept by ROTC Cadet Company E-Z.

Rich Clarkson

above

■ TEXAS A&M VS. TEXAS

Texas' famed Bevo,
a longhorn steer,
stands his ground in
the end zone of every
UT game as have his
12 predecessors.
The steers are handled
by the men of the
honorary Silver Spurs.

Rich Clarkson

left

■ ARMY VS. COLGATE

Cadets aren't the
only ones who get
GI-issue haircuts.
Army's mule has the
military academy's
emblem shaved into
its flanks.

Neil Leifer

■ OREGON VS. OREGON STATE

Juan Navarro, Oregon
State's beaver, and
Scott Sobell, Oregon's
duck, pose in and out
of their Disneyesque
mascot outfits.

Brian Lanker

■ CBS PRODUCTION TRUCK

In the dim glow of television monitors, switcher Jeff Court (left), director Joe Aceti (center) and producer Michael Burks put together a live telecast.

Rich Clarkson

When you grow up in Ohio, the idea of a football game played in full, unchecked sunshine beneath fluttering palms on New Year's Day is an act of faith. There is no possible reality to it, but conditioned by ritual, you believe it nonetheless. The Ohio wind whistles outside your door, perhaps piling drifts of snow against it in the growing darkness. And in the Rose Bowl, a shirt-sleeved crowd watches a football game beneath full, unchecked sunshine. You make a resolution: That's where you'll go.

How many midwesterners have been thus converted? There is no telling, although the popular history is that the Rose Bowl activities, parade and game, were conceived as just the kind of extravagant flyer, a complicated land promotion, to draw shivering masses to Pasadena, a town that was itself a Midwest invention (the dominating Gamble family was of Cincinnati). How could the game work otherwise? And with TV taking the place of the postcard, the concept became even more convincing: blue skies behind the San Gabriel mountains, the wealth of climate and scenery promising equal returns in opportunity and experience.

In the decade since I arrived from Ohio, I do not remember the Rose Bowl stinting in that illusion. It may have rained New Year's morning. Perhaps as recently as the day before, the San Gabriels were fouled by a cloud of pollutants. The traffic to and from was certainly nightmarish. But by game time, as some rightfully wary team from the Midwest began testing the stadium floor, the conditions of sunshine and clarity and order were inevitably restored. A pregame show might reveal the fans sprawled on the grassy arroyo floor, framed by hillsides of bougainvillea. Back in Ohio, a young boy would lean forward in disbelief.

I cannot tell you who played that first game I attended a decade ago. What I remember is a terrific and violent shaking that reached me high in the press box. It was as if the 100,000 shirt-sleeved fans had suddenly begun pounding their feet the way high school kids will do on wooden bleachers. It was an earthquake, my first. A decade later an earthquake would visit a California game site with far more tragic results. But this one was considered strictly for its entertainment value, and it was my definite impression that the crowd was more thrilled than frightened by this pre-game show. (This impression was certainly validated sometime later when a nearby theme park incorporated the sensation into a ride.) A parade, a football game, an earthquake. A pretty good day all in all.

Tom Jagoe/Los Angeles Daily News

For a certain personality this type of experience—one attraction piled onto another—was more threatening than satisfying. I'm thinking of my fellow midwesterners, the ones who came to visit but would never stay. I guess I'm thinking of men like Woody and Bo, and the boys they molded, arriving reluctant but determined. The evidence is, they hated it. The Big Ten teams remain conservative, both in their football and in their lifestyle, and the flamboyance of the West was an affront. The West Coast teams passed wildly, for one thing. A UCLA coach who had been winning regularly with ordinary (that is, Big Ten style) offenses switched to a throwing game simply because the press and fans demanded more excitement for their entertainment dollar. More than that, there wasn't a pre-game event the West Coast boys wouldn't attend. Yet every year, the teams arriving generally on Christmas day, Bo or Woody would declaim these extravagances and announce a new and lower threshold of distractions. No Disneyland. No Beef Bowl. Or no press.

They generally lost anyway, their degree of futility given a comic edge by a coach's temper tantrum. Even when Woody punched a photographer, or Bo became especially vitriolic, it was possible to be sympathetic. What possible chance did they have in a land of earthquakes, bougainvillea and theme parks? In the West, hard work was not only not enough, it may have been irrelevant. Variety of experience was the point for all the pioneers here. For goodness sakes, a coach discarded a perfectly good offense because it bored the team's fans.

Do you really wonder why they hated it here? The Rose Bowl seemed to enforce every midwesterner's worst stereotype of California. The next Rose Bowl game I attended was Michigan-USC. There were no natural disasters, except from Bo's point of view. Late in the game, on another gorgeous afternoon,

Trojan tailback Charles White, who would later wither in Cleveland as a pro (this works both ways), scored the winning touchdown without the encumbrance of a football. Bo was properly apoplectic. The Trojan coach could barely stifle his amusement. It seemed like he scored, and illusion goes a long way in these parts. You can imagine the midwesterners returning home and explaining this to their neighbors: I tell you, it's a fantasy factory out there—even their football is staged for effect.

In those 10 years, of course, the Big Ten teams won a few games. Even Bo, whose career was otherwise exemplary except for postseason play, managed to avoid a shutout. But they were always outsiders, distrustful and resentful. They couldn't wait to go back to Ann Arbor or Columbus, where college football was the proper focus of a community, where there was no competition for the fan's imagination, where matters were exactly as they seemed, where hard work counted more than style.

Myung Chun/Los Angeles Daily News

Bo's last game as a head coach came, fittingly enough, in the Rose Bowl. Even in Southern California there seemed to be some support for a Michigan victory, just because it conformed to Hollywood's standards for a happy ending: Gruff coach finally leaves game a winner, hoisted by his players above an unforgiving turf. You know how it came out, though. And if there's a scene that will stay with me, it's Bo violently protesting an official's call, getting tangled up with some wires and falling to the ground, his clipboard held high. The sheer fury of his protest allowed some dignity to an otherwise childish temper tantrum. But it seemed to me he went out pretty much the way he came in: He never did get it.

Leaving the Rose Bowl that day, I was amused to find it had begun to drizzle. The skies were darkening, and the traffic was typically terrible. Of course, the cameras had long since been turned off, and a picture postcard of sunny skies and fluttering palm trees remained unspoiled in many imaginations deep in the heartland. I though for sure there had to be a boy back in Ohio, his head filled to bursting with this fantasy, resolving to come here, where anything but Big Ten football was possible. Come on.

■ USC vs. UCLA

Hollywood photographer Douglas Kirkland, who set out to portray the sexual side of college football, noted that "women weren't embarrassed to tell me about their fascination with looking at players' bodies."

Douglas Kirkland

■ EASTERN NEW MEXICO STATE

Everett Hood, cornerback,
5 feet 9 inches, 185 pounds.

Michael O'Brien

■ EASTERN NEW MEXICO STATE

Mike Sinclair, defensive end,
6 feet 4 inches, 245 pounds.

Michael O'Brien

COACH

Photography by Brian Lanker

No game day is more special to the coach than the post-season bowl, for it is both a measure of accomplishment at season's end and a kickoff to the next year. A bowl game victory translates into many benefits—including advantages in recruiting players. With plenty of time to spare before his night game, Oregon coach Rich Brooks whiles away the hours before the Independence Bowl in Shreveport, Louisiana.

■ In the hotel room, Brooks watches a professional game on television. His wife, Karen, shows a newspaper picture of their daughter from the previous night's pep rally.

■ The team boards the bus and heads for the stadium, where Brooks obliges a request for a TV interview. Tulsa had capitalized on Oregon turnovers early in the game, and Brooks has tough words for his team before the second half.

■ The Ducks scored 17 unanswered points to win the game 27-24, and even 20-degree temperatures couldn't stop Brooks' team from dousing him. After he was carried from the field, the coach took his team back to the Oregon side to salute their fans.

■ In the locker room, the celebration included a short speech by Oregon governor Neil Goldschimdt, enlivened by Karen Brooks' sneaking in for a hug and a kiss. Brooks later led the team in a cheer for quarterback Bill Musgrave, winner of the MVP trophy. After the press conference, the interviews and the congratulations of many friends, an exhausted Brooks shared a quiet moment with Steve Hellyer, the school's sports information director.

right

■ TEXAS A&M VS. TEXAS

Texas A&M's honor guard sends a traditional yell from the sidelines, "humping it," as the crouched stance is called, to better project their voices. A&M was organized as a military school in 1876, but today only 2,000 of the school's 40,000 students are in ROTC.

Rich Clarkson

following pages

■ HOWARD VS. FLORIDA A&M

Florida A&M tuba players check their instruments before halftime, when they will be the "rattle" in the formation that represents the school's mascot, the rattlesnake. The high knee lifts, dance steps and "techniques of relevancy" are the creation of Dr. William Foster, their director since 1946.

Neil Leifer

THE GAME

Finally, the practice, the travel, the waiting, the interviews and the warmups are over. It's time for the game. Long before there were bands and boosters, television and tailgate parties, the main event was on the field, 11 young men against 11 others.

■ STANFORD VS. CAL
Stanford players relax on the team bus taking them only a few blocks off campus to Ricky's Hyatt House—the hotel where they spend Friday night before the game away from the hubbub of the campus. This is a common practice for college teams which enables coaches to eliminate distractions and manage the hours before a game.

George Olson

 NEBRASKA VS. OKLAHOMA

A lineman's-eye view reveals the hazards of the interior game.

Kenneth Jarecke

right

■ NEBRASKA VS. OKLAHOMA

Oklahoma quarterback Steve Collins tries a move on Nebraska safety Reggie Cooper.

Kenneth Jarecke

■ NOTRE DAME VS. USC

After Notre Dame senior quarterback Tony Rice dives for a score, tailback Ricky Waters celebrates.

Rich Clarkson

preceding pages

■ MICHIGAN VS. OHIO STATE

Ohio State fullback Scottie Graham churns toward the Wolverine line.

Rich Clarkson

above

■ BRIGHAM YOUNG VS.
OREGON STATE

BYU defensive tackle
Rich Kaufusi hoists his
helmet in celebration
of victory after a
fourth-quarter rally.

Jim Richardson

left

■ NOTRE DAME VS. USC

Notre Dame players
raise their helmets to
salute the student
section, a tradition
after every home win.

Rich Clarkson

■ USC vs. UCLA

The locker room is
not always the scene
of joyous celebration.
As the sportswriters
and broadcasters
cluster around, UCLA
quarterback Brett
Johnson reappraises
the game. Defensive
lineman Jon Pryor
will leave the stadium
this day with the help
of crutches.

Douglas Kirkland

■ NEBRASKA VS. OKLAHOMA

Swept up by the emotion of the moment, offensive tackle Tom Punt helps Nebraska fans pull down the goal posts after the Cornhuskers' victory over Oklahoma. Later, a groundskeeper examines the hole where the goal post stood.

Kenneth Jarecke

■ INDIANA VS. PURDUE

The Heisman Trophy is the highest award a college player can win. Going into the final game of the season, Anthony Thompson was the odds-on favorite. All he needed was a great final game. Indiana, by defeating Purdue, would be invited to the Freedom Bowl. But it was not to be: Indiana lost by one point, and Thompson lost the Heisman. In the locker room, coach Bill Mallory consoled him after the game.

William Strode

■ HOUSTON VS. RICE

One week later, Houston quarterback Andre Ware insisted that his offensive line be with him as he watched the live announcement of the Heisman Trophy winner. He earned the trophy by setting 17 NCAA records.

Jay Dickman

THE PHOTOGRAPHERS

Bill Eppridge

SAM ABELL

Sam Abell began photography under the guidance of his father in Sylvania, Ohio, and so he jumped at the opportunity to cover the Ohio State-Michigan game. He also photographed a University of Virginia game close to his Crozet, Virginia, home. Since 1972, Abell's poetic images have been regularly featured in *National Geographic*. Among his publications are two books on the Civil War, and *C.M. Russell's West*, an exploration of the land of one of America's most gifted Western artists. A photograph from his story on Tolstoy's Russia became the theme picture of the 100th anniversary collection of *National Geographic* photography, *Odyssey*. The subject of a video program, "The Art of Simplicity," and a much sought-after leader of photography workshops, Abell has recently gathered his work in a retrospective monograph entitled *Stay This Moment*.

WILLIAM ALBERT ALLARD

Allard's book on the American cowboy, *Vanishing Breed*, is a contemporary classic, and his recently published retrospective, *William Albert Allard: The Photographic Essay*, reveals his versatility. A Minnesota native, Allard attended the Minneapolis School of Fine Arts and the University of Minnesota. After college, a summer internship at the *National Geographic* turned into a full-time contract. Those first years at the magazine took him from climbing Canada's Mount Kennedy with Bobby Kennedy to a tour of America with Lynda Bird Johnson. Other assignments have led him to Peru, Mexico, Australia and France. Recently, his fascination with William Faulkner's Mississippi resulted in a memorable *National Geographic* story with Willie Morris.

JOSE AZEL

Azel is one of three GAME DAY USA photographers associated with Contact Press Images, Inc., a New York agency known for its artistic photojournalism. Azel chose to travel with the Maine University football team to its game with Boston University, and he was quickly accepted into the team meetings and locker rooms. As an undergraduate, he was on Cornell University's track and lightweight football

teams. Today, he is an accomplished mountain climber. Azel, Cuban born, received a masters degree in journalism from the University of Missouri. His work appears regularly in *Time*, *Sports Illustrated*, *Smithsonian*, *National Geographic*, *Connoisseur*, the *London Sunday Times*, and *Geo*.

DAVID BURNETT

Burnett has made some of the most memorable photographs of the Olympics. His portfolio of the Seoul games for *Life* magazine won awards, but he is probably best known for his picture of the grief-stricken Mary Decker Slaney after her collision at the Los Angeles games in 1984. Burnett, a native of Salt Lake City, studied political science at Colorado College, but he had photography assignments for *Time* magazine even then. In 1979, his coverage of the Iranian revolution and behind-the-scenes pictures of the Ayatollah Khomeini garnered many awards, including the Overseas Press Club award for the best foreign photographic reporting of the year and the National Press Photographers Association "Magazine Photographer of the Year" prize. Burnett cofounded Contact Press Images with Robert Pledge.

RICH CLARKSON

Clarkson began photography while in junior high school, and by the time he graduated from the University of Kansas, he was on assignment for *Sports Illustrated*. While continuing there as a contributing photographer, he has devoted most of his time to non-sports photography— as director of photography for the National Geographic Society, assistant managing editor/graphics of the *Denver Post*, and for 22 years, as director of photography of the *Topeka (Ks.) Capital-Journal*. He has had assignments from many national magazines and has covered seven Olympics. Clarkson, the producer of GAME DAY USA, has produced four other sports books (on the Olympics, Oklahoma football, Indiana basketball, and the NCAA basketball championships), and was director of photography for *A Day in the Life of America* in 1986.

JAY DICKMAN

Dickman studied English literature at the University of Texas at Arlington and began his work in photography at the same time. In 1970, he joined the staff of the *Dallas Times-Herald,* one of the premier photojournalistic newspapers in the nation. Dickman's images of El Salvador won the Pulitzer Prize

for news photography in 1983. He joined the staff of the *Denver Post* three years later and eventually went into business on his own, dealing principally in editorial photography for such magazines as *National Geographic*, *Life* and *Fortune*. His work has been featured in seven *Day in the Life* books.

DAN DRY

Dry attended Ohio University in his home town of Athens at the height of the Woody Hayes era in Columbus, and he soon acquired the assignment of photographing Ohio State games for the local newspaper. In the years since college, Dry moved from sports into many other specialties, beginning as a staff photographer at the *Louisville Courier-Journal*, where many prizes culminated with "Newspaper Photographer of the Year" in 1982. He left the newspaper to open his own business, working primarily on corporate advertisements and annual reports, but has kept his hand firmly in editorial photography through work for such magazines as *National Geographic*, *Time* and *Newsweek*. He has been selected for five *Day in the Life* projects, and he profiles colleges for Harmony House Publishers.

BILL EPPRIDGE

Eppridge is one of a long list of famous graduates of the University of Missouri's School of Journalism, where he won "College Photographer of the Year" as a senior. His first job after graduation was with *National Geographic,* but he was soon hired by *Life* as a staff photographer in 1962. During those years at *Life,* Eppridge's masterful essay on a drug-addicted couple in New York introduced the subject into the American consciousness. Eppridge also covered Robert Kennedy's presidential campaign for *Life*; his most famous photograph is of the mortally wounded Kennedy lying on the floor of the Ambassador Hotel's kitchen. Today, Eppridge is a contract photographer at *Sports Illustrated,* where he specializes in feature essays and stories of fishing, hunting and sailing.

ARTHUR GRACE

Grace is known for his pointed, often humorous pictures from the world of politics, many of them gathered in his recent book, *Choose Me: Portraits of a Presidential Race,* published following the 1988 campaign. Grace attended Bowdoin College and graduated from Brandeis University. He began his career in Boston and Brussels working for United Press International, and then

became a *Time* contract photographer assigned to the Carter White House. In the 1980s, Grace worked out of *Time*'s Warsaw bureau to cover the story of Solidarity and the imposition of martial law in Poland. He joined the staff of *Newsweek* in 1986 and is now a contributing photographer out of their Washington bureau.

KENNETH JARECKE

Jarecke, a member of the Contact Press Images photo agency, was a student at the University of Nebraska at Omaha, where he played nose-guard on the football team. Jarecke's return to Nebraska to photograph the Oklahoma-Nebraska game was a real home-coming; his first job out of college was covering Nebraska football for the Associated Press. Today, he photographs for many international magazines, and his work is probably more familiar to the readers of *Stern, Sette,* and *Paris Match* than to Americans, although he does regular assignments for *Life* and *Time.* He has covered the student demonstrations in China, the Iran-Contra hearings, the 1988 American presidential campaign and the Malta Summit.

LYNN JOHNSON

When Johnson first examined the pictures of Dorothea Lange, one of the group of FSA photographers who documented the Depression Era, photography for her turned from a hobby into a passion. She enrolled in the Rochester Institute of Technology, majoring in photojournalism and illustration, which led to her first professional job in 1975 at the *Pittsburgh Press.* Her probing and sympathetic essays have earned her many awards, including the Robert F. Kennedy Prize for outstanding coverage of the disadvantaged. Her story for *Life* magazine on breast reconstruction won praise for helping women through difficult times. She is now affiliated with the Black Star agency, and her work appears regularly in *Life, Fortune, Newsweek, Forbes* and *National Geographic.*

R. EMMETT JORDAN

When Jordan was editor of the yearbook at the University of Colorado, the football team was going nowhere. But for GAME DAY USA, he was able to photograph one of the nation's best squads. After graduation, Jordan worked at newspapers in Denver, Tucson, Los Angeles and Boulder before becoming photography editor and department head at the *Sarasota (Fla.) Herald-Tribune.* He returned to Denver in 1989 and worked as associate producer of GAME DAY USA.

NICK KELSH

As a teenager growing up in Fargo, Kelsh spent Saturday afternoons hawking popcorn at North Dakota State University football games. When he selected his project for GAME DAY USA, it was back to visit the grounds of the "Thundering Herd." Kelsh left North Dakota for journalism school at Missouri, which led to a stint as a staff photographer on the *Columbia Daily Tribune.* He moved to Philadelphia to work primarily for the weekly magazine of the *Philadelphia Inquirer,* but left to join with Bill Marr (the art director of GAME DAY USA) to open a design and photography studio specializing in corporate publications and annual reports. He has participated in several *Day in the Life* projects, and he produced the cover image for *A Day in the Life of China.*

ROBB KENDRICK

The 26-year-old Kendrick was born in Nebraska but later moved to small-town Texas. He attended East Texas State University before going to Houston to assist Joe Baraban, a corporate and advertising photographer. Kendrick left to take a summer internship at the *National Geographic* magazine, returning to

George Olson

Houston to start out on his own. He has worked on a variety of books, including two in the *Day in the Life* series, and has been published in *National Geographic, Life, Geo, Travel and Leisure* and *Newsweek.*

DOUGLAS KIRKLAND

Perhaps the most famous contemporary Hollywood photographer, Kirkland is a native Canadian. Early in his career, he became an apprentice to *Vogue* photographer Irving Penn, which led to a staff position with *Look* magazine. In 1971, he joined the staff of *Life* and lived in New York for 15 years before moving to Hollywood, where much of his work was taking place. A friend and confidant of many Hollywood stars over the years, he has recently published *Douglas Kirkland's Light Years—Three Decades of Photographing the Stars.* His pictures appear in magazines around the world and are often used as poster art for motion pictures, including *Out of Africa* and *Sophie's Choice.*

Rich Clarkson

Douglas Kirkland

BRIAN LANKER

Before 1989, Lanker was probably best known for his *Sports Illustrated* swimsuit issues. But his book and traveling exhibition, *I Dream a World*, portraits in pictures and words of America's most respected black women, has redirected his career. A project over three years in the making, the exhibition attracts record crowds in museums and art galleries across the nation and is booked into 1993. Lanker's portraits and essays in *Sports Illustrated* and *Life* in recent years follow a career in newspapers in the 1970s, when he won the Pulitzer Prize in feature photography and became one of only five photographers to win the national "Newspaper Photographer of the Year" award twice.

NEIL LEIFER

At 17, Leifer parlayed his delicatessen delivery route at *Sports Illustrated* into an assignment to cover a New York Giants football game. In the years that followed, Leifer's pictures appeared on 152 covers, and he became one of America's most prolific and best-known sports photographers. Leifer moved to the staff of *Time* in 1978, where he has flourished in the nonsports world with more than 30 covers; he also photographs for *Life*. A director of two feature-length films, Leifer is fascinated with the production of motion pictures and has done special photography for *The Longest Yard, Semi-Tough, Chariots of Fire, One From the Heart* and *F.I.S.T.* His books include *Sports* and *Neil Leifer's Sports Stars*.

JOHN LOENGARD

Often described as "the thinking man's photographer," John Loengard is known for his careful technique and unique approach. He was given his first *Life* assignment while a senior at Harvard, joining the staff two years later. *American Photographer* hailed him as *Life*'s most influential photographer during the 1960s. His essays "The Shakers" (1967), "Georgia O'Keefe" (1968) and "The Vanishing Cowboy" (1970) are all considered classics. After the closing of *Life* weekly, he became the first picture editor of *People*. Instrumental in the rebirth of *Life* as a monthly, he served as its picture editor for nine years. His two recent books have been much acclaimed; the first, *Pictures Under Discussion,* analyzes his own photographs, while the recent *Life Classic Photographs: A Personal Interpretation* considers the work of others.

MICHAEL O'BRIEN

O'Brien began his career at the University of Tennessee covering football for the *U.T. Daily Beacon*. Fresh out of college with a degree in philosophy, he took a job at the now-defunct *Miami News,* where his pictures attracted national attention. While there, he twice won the Robert F. Kennedy journalism award for coverage of the disadvantaged. He left the newspaper in 1979 to begin freelancing from New York, where he does assignments for such diverse publications as the *London Sunday Times Magazine, Esquire* and *National Geographic*.

GEORGE OLSON

Today a freelance photographer in San Francisco, Olson began his career in Topeka, Kansas, where he won the title "College Photographer of the Year" while a student at Washburn University. He worked for newspapers in Topeka and Kansas City before relocating to the West Coast in 1977. He photographs for corporate clients and does editorial work for *National Geographic, Sports Illustrated* and *Smithsonian*. Olson, whose photographs often evoke subtle humor, gave special attention to the Stanford band.

JIM RICHARDSON

Richardson, who freelances from Denver, has held staff positions at the *Topeka Capital-Journal*, the *Omaha World-Herald* and the *Denver Post*. Hearkening to his days in a one-room schoolhouse in north-central Kansas, Richardson has documented small-town America for the past 15 years. His project has been published in a variety of forms: *American Photographer* ran his images as their longest essay ever; a multi-projector audio-visual show has won numerous prizes; and a version was aired on "CBS Sunday Morning." His books include *High School USA* and four college profiles in the Harmony House series. He has been published in four of the *Day in the Life* projects.

WILLIAM STRODE

Strode has been a catalyst in American photojournalism, serving as assistant director of photography of the *Louisville Courier-Journal and Times* and as president of the National Press Photographers Association in 1974. He has won numerous awards, including "Newspaper Photographer of the Year" in 1966 as well as World Press and Overseas Press Club prizes. He shared in two Pulitzer Prizes awarded the staff of the *Courier-Journal* during his tenure. Today, Strode is president of his own photography business and co-owner of Harmony House Publishing.

THE WRITERS

FRANK CONROY

A graduate of Haverford College, Conroy taught at M.I.T., Brandeis and George Mason University before becoming director of the famed Iowa Writers' Workshop. He has also served as director of the literature program of the National Endowment for the Arts. Conroy's books include the highly acclaimed *Stop Time* and *Midair*. He was a contributor to *Smiling Through the Apocalypse: Esquire's History of the '60s* and has written for the *New York Times Magazine*, the *Chicago Tribune*, *Boston Magazine*, the *New Yorker* and *Harper's*.

DAVID HALBERSTAM

As managing editor of the *Harvard Crimson*, David Halberstam was an occasional sportswriter. After his graduation in 1955, he quickly distinguished himself as a foreign correspondent; assignments for the *New York Times* took him to Vietnam, where his prophetic reporting earned him the Pulitzer Prize in 1964 and led to his first book, *The Making of a Quagmire*.

Halberstam's dozen award-winning books include the classic series on power in America, *The Best and the Brightest*, *The Powers That Be* and *The Reckoning*. Recently, he has turned to the relationship of sports to American culture with *The Breaks of the Game*, about professional basketball, *The Amateurs*, about Olympic rowing, and *Summer of '49*, about a classic baseball season. He also contributes to *Esquire*, the *Atlantic Monthly*, *McCalls* and *Harper's*.

RICHARD HOFFER

Hoffer's first job out of Miami of Ohio was typing bowling scores for the *Massilon (Ohio) Evening Independent*. After two years, he entered Stanford for a masters in journalism. Following graduation, Hoffer wrote for newspapers in Ohio and California before joining the *Los Angeles Times*, where his coverage during the 1984 Olympic Games won many prizes, including the *Sporting News'* award for the Best Reporting Story of 1984. He now contributes special features as a staff writer for *Sports Illustrated*.

WILLIE MORRIS

Morris grew up in Yazoo City, Mississippi, where he played outfield for the semipro Yazoo City Screaming Eagles. At the University of Texas, he was editor-in-chief of the *Daily Texan* and won a Rhodes Scholarship to Oxford University. He edited the *Texas Observer* from 1960-63 before becoming editor of *Harper's*, from which he and most of the staff resigned in 1971 in a celebrated editorial dispute. In 1980, he returned to "the other Oxford" as a writer in residence at the University of Mississippi. His award-winning memoir, *North Toward Home*, was followed by *Yazoo: Integration in a Deep South Town*, *Good Old Boy*, a children's novel later made into a Disney movie, *The Last of the Southern Girls* and *James Jones: A Friendship*. His most famous sports book, *The Courting of Marcus Dupree*, is a Christopher Medal-winning account of the recruiting of Neshoba County, Mississippi's best-ever high school football player.

Sam Abell

ACKNOWLEDGEMENTS

The idea for GAME DAY USA evolved from planning sessions for the Visitors Center in the new NCAA office complex in Kansas City, and Bob Sprenger, the NCAA assistant executive director in charge of the Center, originally put the project in perspective. Bob and his assistant, Will Rudd, put in many hours of encouragement and advice, opening doors and making invaluable introductions.

No less instrumental at the beginning of the project was the visionary vice president of the Eastman Kodak Company, Raymond H. DeMoulin. Under his leadership, the Professional Photography Division has stepped forward to insure that countless good-idea projects get started. John Grant and Frank Thomasson were quick to bring together the experience and excellence of their company to join with Kodak in their first joint publishing venture—GAME DAY USA.

As the team came together, everyone tackled his part as a labor of love. Bill Marr's wonderful disposition and great talent as a designer were the perfect accompaniment to the insightful picture editing of Susan Vermazen of *New York* magazine and Peter Howe of *Life* magazine. My associate, R. Emmett Jordan, contributed at every stage of the project and took some fine pictures. Good advice and counsel came from Brian Lanker, Neil Leifer, R. Smith Schuneman, Sean Callahan and Howard Chapnick. At Thomasson-Grant, Rebecca Beall Barns, Hoke Perkins and Leonard Phillips helped produce the book.

Thanks also go to many at the NCAA, including executive director Dick Schultz, assistants David Cawood and Tom Jernstedt and staff members Kelly Fray and Sherry Nelson. And to Charles Neinas, executive director of the College Football Association, and his assistant for television, David Ogrean.

More good advice came from Mark Mulvoy, managing editor of *Sports Illustrated*, his director of photography, Karen Mullarkey, and her assistant, Phil Jache.

Technical support and logistical help came from Richard Mackson of Westside Processing, John S. Harcourt of Nikon Inc. and Pete Zogas of National Instruments. Others included Chris Adams, Brian Wilkinson, Curtis Hilburn, Jeff Harrington and Ace Allgood.

There was also Steve Hatchell, executive director of the Orange Bowl, basketball coaches Bob Knight of Indiana and Richard "Digger" Phelps of Notre Dame, football coaches Jack Bicknell of Boston College, Bill Mallory of Indiana, R.C. Slocum of Texas A&M, John Mackovic of Illinois, Eddie Robinson of Grambling, Glen Mason of Kansas and Bill McCartney of Colorado. Many people helped at the schools, including:

Rich Murray, University of Virginia; Tim Bourret, Clemson University; George Ellis, North Dakota State University; Budd Thalman, Penn State University; Langston Rogers, University of Mississippi; Greg Seiter, Gallaudet University; William Steinman, Columbia University; Ian McCaw, University of Maine; Ed Carpenter, Boston University; John Roth, Duke University; Wendel Sloan, Eastern New Mexico University; Peter Moore, Ithaca College; Ralph Zobell, Brigham Young University; Dave Plati, University of Colorado;

Dave Senko, University of Washington; Tim Tessalone, University of Southern California; Tom Simons and Don Bryant, University of Nebraska; Edward Hill, Howard University; Stanley Lewis, Grambling State University; Steve Raczynski, Stanford University; Steve Ulrich, Yale University; Alan Cannon, Texas A&M University; Bob Kinney, United States Military Academy; Tom Bates, United States Naval Academy; Dave Kellogg, United States Air Force Academy; Bruce Madej and Will Perry, Michigan University;

David Housel, Auburn University; Roger Valdiserri and John Heisler, Notre Dame University; Ed Wisneski, Southern Methodist University; Alvin Hollins, Florida A&M University; Jim Muldoon, Pacific-10 Conference; Reid Oslin, Boston College; Lonza Hardy, Jr., Southern University & A&M; Mike Pearson and Dave Johnson, University of Illinois; Kit Klingelhoffer, Indiana University, and Linda Venzon, University of Pittsburgh; Doug Vance, University of Kansas.   —*Rich Clarkson*

■ BRIGHAM YOUNG
VS. OREGON

The sun doesn't set in Provo before the cleanup of the Brigham Young stadium.

Jim Richardson